My details

Name: ______________________________

School: ______________________________

Friends: ______________________________

Interests: ______________________________

____

____

____

Before you begin writing ...

Here are the 3**P**s that will help you with your writing: **p**osture, **p**encil grip and **p**aper position. You will be reminded about these as you go through the book.

Posture

1. Sit up straight at your table.
2. Put your feet flat on the floor.
3. Keep your wrist straight and resting on the table.

Pencil or pen grip

1. Rest the pencil or pen on your middle finger.
2. Pinch your index finger and thumb together gently.

Left-handed

Right-handed

Paper

1. The paper is on an angle and held steady by your non-writing hand.
2. For right-handers, the page will tilt to the left.
3. For left-handers, the page will tilt to the right.

Left-handed

Right-handed

OXFORD UNIVERSITY PRESS

Revision

Printing

Before you begin, complete the checklist below.

- ❏ I have my feet flat on the floor.
- ❏ My back is up nice and straight.
- ❏ I can hold the pencil or pen correctly.

Consolidate your printing of lower-case letters.

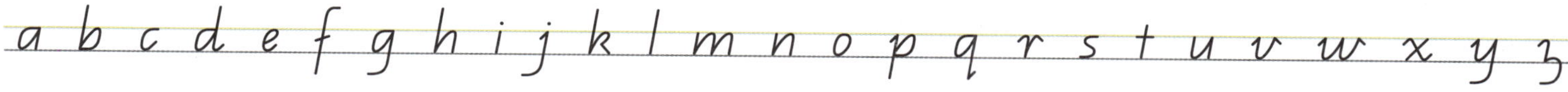

Consolidate your printing of capital letters.

Consolidate your numerals and punctuation marks.

Finish the table below. The first one is done for you.

55 489	Fifty-five thousand, four hundred and eighty-nine
5632	
15 311	
5 110 000	
506 210	
50 766	

Copy the sentences below.

Participating in regular physical activity is good for your health. It is important to find physical activities that you enjoy. This can include playing a sport or other types of active lifestyle habits, such as walking, hiking, gardening or yoga.

Copy these words

bike riding

skateboarding

jogging

stretching

physical

gardening

Diagonal joins

Learning intention:
To revise diagonal joins when forming letters

What are diagonal joins?

in eu

A diagonal join is made from the bottom of one letter to the top of the next letter.

Practise these diagonal joins.

am an ap ar at ay ce cr di dr dy he hu

in is le li me mi ni nu te ti un uc ix ki

Diagonal joins occur when one letter smoothly transitions to another at an angle. Try not to lift your pencil or pen.

Move along the path without going over the edges.

Trace over these letter combinations and then copy them on the lines below. Remember not to lift your pencil or pen.

ni ni ni eu eu eu ne ne ne

ep ep ep mi mi mi nu nu nu

di di di ip ip ip li li li

Use diagonal joins to practise these sentences.

An active lifestyle includes regular physical activity

and healthy eating. This means making an effort

to be active throughout the day.

Word building!

heal

Meaning: to cure or save; make whole, sound and well (from Old English)

Using the base word "heal", how many words can you form?

For example: heal + th = health

Don't forget: we often change the y at the end of a word to an i before adding the suffix.

Prefix	Base word	Suffixes			List your words here
un-	heal	-s -ing -ed -er			
		-th	-y	-er -est -ly -ness	

Practising diagonal joins

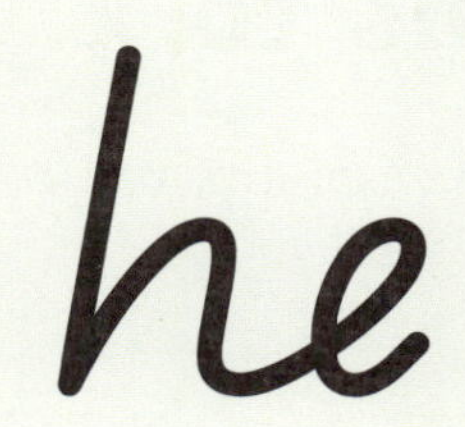

Learning intention: To practise diagonal joins

Copy these letter pairs and the paragraph on the lines below.

he te me ae ce ne is de ee ke le ue

Participating in sport can have a powerful impact on children, as it gives them the chance to develop physical capabilities and teamwork skills. They also learn the value of dedicated practice. Children who are passionate about their sport persevere through challenges, have unwavering commitment and strive for excellence. There are ball sports, such as cricket, table tennis, basketball and football. Other sports include swimming, dancing and athletics. Keep trying until you find what you enjoy doing.

Joins to x

Practise your joins to and from x.

Always cross the letter x before you write the next letter.

xa xi xe

Trace and then copy these joins to and from x.

xa xe xi xo xu ax ex ix ox ux

Trace and then copy these words with joins to and from x.

exercise exploration extreme next relax

excitement wax boxer exactly excellence

Write your own sentence using some of the words on this page with the letter x.

Diagonal joins to tall letters

Learning intention:
To practise diagonal joins to tall letters

I am successful when I can:
- ❑ sit with my back straight
- ❑ hold the pencil or pen correctly
- ❑ position my paper
- ❑ make diagonal joins smoothly.

A diagonal join is made from the bottom of a lower-case letter to a tall letter.

Use a sweeping movement to practise writing these diagonal joins to tall letters.

al th et ub cl ch nk it el ul lt lk at

Tip! The crossbar on t sits a bit higher than the letter body.

activities

fitness

nutrient

active

stretch

Practise these diagonal joins to tall letters.

Playing a sport is a great way of keeping fit and healthy.

There are a variety of sports and activities to engage in.

Regular physical activity has many health benefits.

Word building!

Add the suffix -ing to the words below.

Remember to drop the e before adding -ing.

If the last letter is a consonant and comes after a vowel, double the consonant before adding -ing (for example, swimming).

The first one is done for you.

swim	swimming	hurdle	
ride		wrestle	
drop		bike	
bounce		run	
skate		cycle	
dance		hop	
jog		jump	

Fine motor skills task: Help Ava through the maze to find her ball. Be careful not to touch the edges or lift your pencil or pen.

Practise keeping your letters on the lines. Make sure you keep the size consistent.

good example

Being active is fun

example of what to avoid

Being active is fun

Playing a sport isn't the only way to stay fit and healthy.

Participating in a hobby or recreational activity that

involves physical movement is also beneficial for your

wellbeing. This could be walking, dancing, hiking,

gardening or taking a yoga class. Select activities you

enjoy that get you moving, and then do them regularly.

Self-assessment Draw a star next to your best writing. Think about size, slope and how well you completed your diagonal joins.

Practise your keyboarding skills by typing the above passage.

Drop-in joins

Learning intention:
To revise drop-in joins

When we do a diagonal join to an anti-clockwise letter, the exit from the first letter reaches high towards the top of the next letter. We then drop the next letter in place.

Drop-in joins help to make smooth transitions from the ending stroke of one letter to the starting stroke of the next letter. This avoids retracing and makes cursive handwriting more legible and elegant.

Extend exit, lift and drop in the next letter.

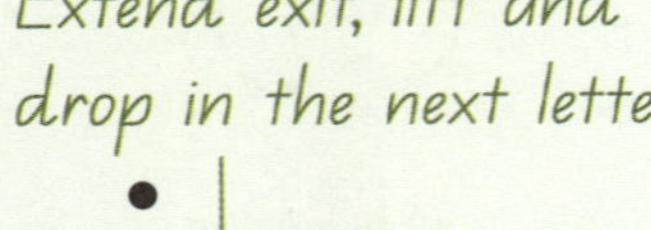

The letters a, c, d, g, o and q are dropped into place. The dot shows you when to lift the pencil or pen.

ac ca dg eq ma da oa ac ca dg ma

Copy these drop-in joins.

na ma ic ud aq ug id eg ec nd da ig uc ag

Practise these drop-in joins.

fantastic sweat exercise start agility light edge

dance posture balance strong conditioning stretch

kick team workout training practise athletic

Self-assessment Underline your smoothest join. Circle a join that needs more practice.

Copy the sentences below, practising your drop-ins and holding your pencil or pen correctly.

Active games and family activities are other fun ways to lead an active lifestyle. Games such as hide and seek, capture the flag, tip and hopscotch are all fun and engaging activities. There are lots of things to do outside in the fresh air. Try bike riding, going for a bush walk or playing a game in the park.

Fine motor skills task: Follow the steps to draw the picture.

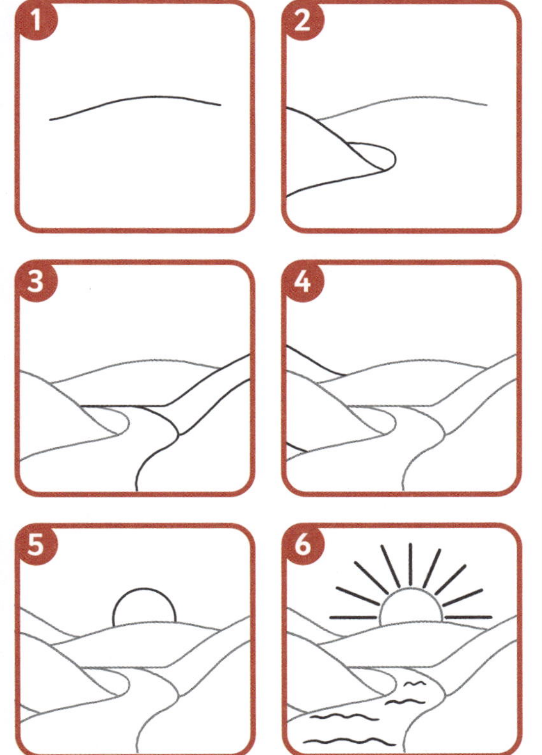

Horizontal joins

Learning intention:
To use horizontal joins for o, r, v and w

small dip — retrace — retrace

or ra ok

Horizontal joins are made from letters that finish near the top. Remember that the letters o, r, v and w do not join to the letter e.

Practise these horizontal joins.

oi om on op or ot ou ov ow ox rb ri rm rn

ru rv rw va vi vo wi wa wn wo oi rp

outings boost workout development explore crucial

Word building!

Build three or more words from the base words, choosing the right suffixes from below. The first one is done for you.

-ment, -ed, -ing, -able, -y, -ive, -ion

Don't forget: we usually drop the e at the end of words when adding a suffix.

excite	excitement	excited	exciting
discover			
participate			
engage			
interact			
cooperate			
coordinate			
enjoy			

Joins from f

Learning intention: To practise joins from the letter f

I am successful when I can:

- ❏ sit with my back straight
- ❏ hold the pencil or pen correctly
- ❏ position my paper
- ❏ make joins from f.

When joining from f, the crossbar is angled.

fr fu fi fr fu from funny friendship fitness

Practise your joins from f by copying these letter pairs and words.

fl fe fl fe flapping flexibility

fa fo fa fo family follow

Fine motor skills task: Draw a picture of you and your family or friends having fun.

Family fun with games and sports is a good way to promote physical activity among family members. Some ideas for family-friendly activities include playing hide and seek, swimming and hiking.

Self-assessment Draw a star next to your best writing. Think about size, slope and how well you completed your joins.

Joins to f

The letter f at the beginning of a word or after a pencil lift looks like this: f

When letters join to f it is written like this: f

If the f is at the start of the word or does not join to the letter before, it is the regular f. When joining to the letter f, remember to loop the f at the top, then lift your pencil or pen to make the angled crossbar.

Practise joining to the letter f by tracing the letters and then copying them.

ef ef ______________ uf uf ______________

af af ______________ if if ______________

surfing often brief mischief careful roof leaf softball

____

Copy the picture of the surfer in the box provided.

OXFORD UNIVERSITY PRESS

Joins to and from f

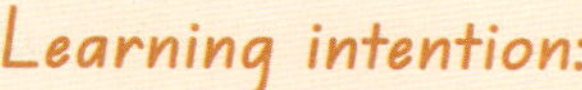

Learning intention:
To practise joins to and from f

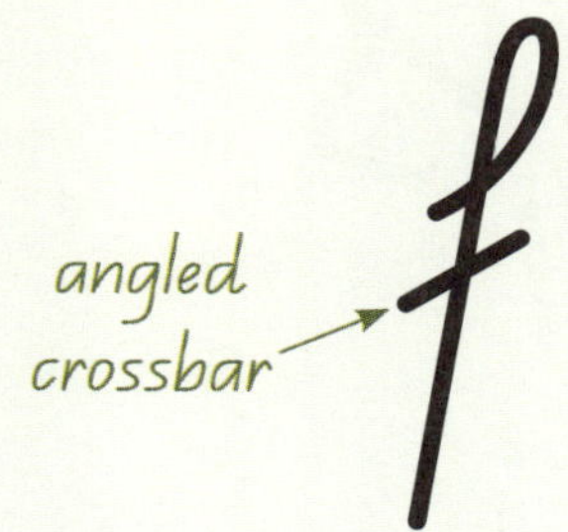

Tip!

Remember that the join from f is angled so it's easier to join to the next letter.

fi

Practise writing the letter f at the beginning of a word.

fa fa fr fr fe fe fi fi fl fl fo fo

field fairness fantastic futsal frisbee

speed loop to f

eft

Practise writing f to and from other letters.

oft oft aft aft ife ife ifu ifu afy afy

leafy beautiful life after before referee often

speed loop at the end of a word

Practise writing when f is the last letter of a word.

ef ef urf urf iff iff uff uff rf rf af af

surf bluff puff self proof chief turf

Joins to s

Learning intention:
To practise horizontal and diagonal joins to s

I am successful when I can:
- ❑ do the 3Ps
- ❑ choose the regular s for horizontal joins, and the short s for diagonal joins.

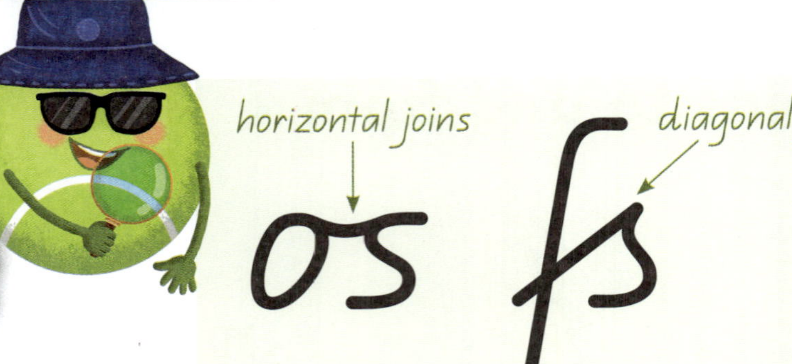

The regular s is used at the start of a word, and also for horizontal joins. When joining diagonally to s, use the short s.

Practise these joins to s.

os rs fs ws us is as ts ls ns us es

lost toss history activities emphasis composes occurs

On the lines below, practise joining the s with a diagonal join, making the top of the s shorter.

Australian sport has a rich and diverse history, with a strong emphasis on outdoor activities and sports.

Copy these words onto the lines below. Underline the words that use a horizontal join to s.

news best muscle stress socks household most

speed members drawstring positive sustain offside

Copy these words with joins to s onto the lines below. Underline the words that use diagonal joins to s.

skates tennis rackets students skills

matches games blossom memories fastest

Which letters always come before a horizontal join to s? ______

Rewrite these words, adding all possible joins.

because ______

most ______

emphasis ______

activities ______

Fine motor skills task: Practise your drawing skills by following these examples.

Learning intention: To develop fluency when writing double s

Joins to double s

I am successful when I can:
- ❑ sit with my back straight
- ❑ hold the pencil or pen correctly
- ❑ position my paper
- ❑ make my double s clear.

horizontal join to s

gloss glass

diagonal join to s

Copy the words below to practise writing double s.

pass bossy motocross toss success lacrosse miss

crossbar dismissal loss wilderness stress breathless

In the game of cricket, a dismissal is when a batter gets out. Common forms of dismissal include being caught, bowled or run out. The outcome of the game may hinge on the toss of the coin, because conditions that one side faces at the start compared to conditions the other side faces later on can dictate the success or struggles for each team throughout the match.

Joins from o, r, v and w

Learning intention:
To practise joins from o, r, v and w

small dip
retrace

or ra

Horizontal joins are made from letters that finish near the top. Remember to add a small dip. These letters do not join to the letter e.

Practise these horizontal joins.

or ra oy oo rt wa od ol va on os vi

ri wn rr ro om ot wd og ov vo rt wi ow

There are many other sports that Australians enjoy, such as basketball, swimming, golf, surfing, cycling and more. Sport plays an important role in Australian culture, by providing entertainment and promoting physical fitness and community engagement.

In cursive handwriting, complete this sentence, adding the correct punctuation mark at the end of the sentence.

My favourite sport is ______________________ because ______________________

Word	Part of speech	Meaning	Image
persevere	verb	To keep trying and not give up, even though it is difficult.	
fervent	adjective	To have strong feelings about something and be very sincere and enthusiastic about it.	
strive	verb	To make a great effort to do or achieve something.	

Use the words "persevere", "fervent" and "strive" as you answer the questions below. Remember to use cursive handwriting.

How do you persevere with a difficult task?

What are you fervent about?

What are you striving to achieve?

Self-assessment

Think about your work in relation to the success criteria.
What did you notice you were able to do well?
What do you need to work on next?

Letters that do not join

As with capital letters, we do not add joins to letters that finish in a clockwise direction. So you can see that b, g, j, p, s, y and z do not join. Can you find them on this page? Practise your cursive handwriting by copying these commonly misspelt words.

achieve		favourite	
library		grateful	
guarantee		believe	
separate		important	
February		definitely	

Copy the text below, remembering that some letters do not join because they finish in a clockwise direction.

Playing a sport gives opportunities to form new

friendships and learn new skills. It also brings joy

and develops a sense of belonging, boosting self-esteem

and improving overall zest and health. Apart from the

benefits to physical health, playing a sport also helps to

build confidence, resilience, pride and a positive attitude.

Consolidating

Diagonal | Drop-in | Horizontal

Extend exit, lift and drop-in the next letter.

small dip

in ia or

Copy the letters below and add the diagonal joins.

ai as an cu in es hi ke ur me

Add joins to these letters. Then underline the drop-in joins and circle the diagonal joins.

ar de ce le ag th ca me ea ua do

Write this sentence adding in joins, including drop-in joins.

Engaging in sport provides quality opportunities for recreation and fun. It also provides a source of leisure and a break from daily routines.

Copy this sentence to practise joining to the letter s.

It is essential to use the correct safety equipment for some sports.

Assessment: Joins

Rewrite these words in cursive, adding in joins where they are needed.

fitness		boost	
because		often	
benefits		promote	
careful		balance	
members		active	
workout		health	
explore		physical	
tennis		soccer	

Copy the passage below to practise your joins.

Sports tourism refers to people travelling to a destination

to participate in or watch a sporting event. For instance,

people might travel to watch sport (such as the Olympics)

or to take part in sports (such as running a marathon).

Teacher feedback

Practise your keyboarding skills by typing this passage.

Practising cursive writing

Becoming a fluent writer

Learning intention:
To develop fluency in joining letters

We will start with some words, and then write paragraphs.

Practise your cursive writing by copying these words.

busy keep several select pride basketball

softball bowling pentathlon powerlifting

sailing pilates baseball applause hobby

ribbon physical platform diving surfing

show jumping blading Olympics athletics

time trials swimming breaking Kierin cycling

amateur sports golfing skiing athletics

OXFORD UNIVERSITY PRESS

Badminton

Badminton is a racket sport played by two or more players. Players use lightweight rackets to strike a shuttlecock. Badminton is played at various skill levels, from backyard games to highly competitive international tournaments.

Softball

Softball is a team sport usually played on a field. It requires a combination of skills, such as batting, throwing, catching and base running. Softball provides great opportunities to develop skills, learn about teamwork and engage in friendly competition.

Netball

Netball is a popular sport incorporating skills such as passing and shooting. Players must work together to pass and catch the ball while trying to outmanoeuvre the other team. The game is played in schools, leagues and at the international level.

Soccer

Soccer is one of Australia's most popular sports. It has a long and rich history in many countries around the world and is sometimes referred to as the "world game". In this fast-paced game, players require skilful footwork, agility and endurance.

More practice for joins with double s

Practise your joins to double s by copying these letters.

oss ess iss uss oss ess iss uss

Practise using cursive handwriting by copying these commonly confused words and their definitions.

lesson – a fixed time when people are taught about a

subject or how to do something

lessen – to become or make something become smaller,

weaker or less important

Fine motor skills task: Follow the steps and complete the drawing.

1

2

3

4

5

6

Consolidating

Copy this passage.

Australian rules football is a fast-paced and physical game. The objective of the game is to score the most points. Goals are worth six points, and behinds are worth one point. A behind is when the ball goes between the behind and goal posts, whereas a goal is when it goes between the two goal posts in the centre. Before Australian rules football, there was the First Nations sport known as marngrook. This game involved kicking and catching a ball made from possum or kangaroo skin.

Teacher feedback

Practise your keyboarding skills by typing this passage.

Assessment: Practising cursive writing

Copy these words to practise your cursive writing.

spectators brave premier strong showcase pitch

bases penalty strike pass sailing blindside

Copy this passage to practise your cursive writing.

People love not only to participate in sport but also to be

spectators. Spectators love watching and cheering on

their favourite teams and sportspeople in a variety of

sports, including swimming, sailing, motocross, tennis,

volleyball and football. Watching sports with other

spectators is exciting and fun. Perhaps more importantly,

it can also provide a sense of belonging and camaraderie.

Draw a star next to your best writing. Think about how well you completed your cursive writing.

Try to write at a steady pace so that your writing is clear and easy to read. Knowing how to spell words correctly makes it easier for your reader as well.

Copy these words, which are commonly misspelt.

jewellery		judgement	
challenge		congratulate	
rhythm		hygiene	
accommodation		specific	
dilemma		separate	

Copy these sentences. Remember that some letters do not join.

The sport of gymnastics is challenging, with athletes needing a combination of strength, agility, flexibility and coordination. Gymnastics dates back thousands of years, with roots in Ancient Greece, where it formed part of the physical training for soldiers.

I am successful when I can:

- ❑ sit with my back straight
- ❑ hold the pencil or pen correctly
- ❑ position my paper
- ❑ increase my fluency and speed.

Write these words in your neatest cursive writing.

The "yellow jersey" is a term used in cycling, particularly in one of the most famous races: the Tour de France. Held annually in July, it has multiple stages, which include flat stages, mountain stages, time trials and more. The rider who wears the yellow jersey at the end of each stage is recognised as the race leader. Wearing the yellow jersey is a significant honour in the sport of cycling and often indicates that the rider is a strong contender to win the overall race.

Practise your keyboarding skills by typing this passage.

Self-assessment Draw a star next to your best writing. Think about size, slope and spacing.

Speed and fluency

Getting faster

Copy these letter pairs, words and sentences on this page and the next.

Learning intention:
To increase fluency and speed when writing

I am successful when I can:
- ❑ increase my speed and fluency when writing these letters.

b b b b ab be ib ob ub bb lb rb bl

able table football tribe able bulb robe

h h h h oh gh ph sh th ch ah oh gh

triathlon shine think marathon workout archery

To enhance their agility and strength, football players work out at the gym. Becoming a football player requires skill, hard work and confidence. Football players work hard to improve their ball handling and kicking skills.

Remember to join your letters correctly, and your fluency will improve.

OXFORD UNIVERSITY PRESS

al cl dl el il gl ll lm ln ol pl rl sl tl

golf cycling athletics goalie walk happily volley

k k k k ak ek ck ok lk nk rk sk uk

walk risk work rink kick jacket kayak strike kit

Copy this sentence, focusing on your speed and fluency.

Soccer, also known as football in many parts of the world, involves a wide range of skills that players need to learn in order to excel. Players need to kick the ball towards the goal and to move swiftly across the field by passing, dribbling and controlling the ball.

Peer feedback

Ask a partner to review your work and provide feedback.

Two stars (two things you did well)

One wish (one suggestion on something you can improve)

Copy these words.

martial wrestling racquetball kiteboarding

mountaineering snowboarding badminton hurdles

Focus on your speed as you copy these words.

bowling		strike	
hockey		pucks	
physical		walking	
kayaking		paddling	
skateboarding		volleyball	
basketball		gymnastics	
boxing		kickboxing	
handball		cricket	

Peer feedback

Ask a partner to review your work and provide feedback.

Two stars (two things you did well)

One wish (one suggestion on something you can improve)

Focus on your speed and fluency as you copy this passage.

The word "football" has different meanings depending on the region you live in. It is a term used to describe a variety of different types of sports involved in kicking a ball to score goals. Around the world, the word "football" is associated with what Australians call soccer. In the United States of America, "football" means a different type of sport, called gridiron. Yard lines divide the field into sections, and the game is played with a combination of passing, running and kicking, with the primary focus being to get the ball into the opponent's end zone to score points.

Practise your cursive writing by copying this passage.

Australia has many sporting champions who have achieved amazing success. A few notable Australian sporting heroes include Donald Bradman, Dawn Fraser, Rod Laver, Raelene Boyle, Evonne Goolagong Cawley, Shane Gould, Cathy Freeman, Ian Thorpe and Dylan Alcott. These are just a few examples of Australian sporting heroes who have made a significant contribution to their sport. Many of these athletes actively engage in their communities through inspirational projects and promoting better outcomes for local causes.

Practise your keyboarding skills by typing this passage.

Self-assessment Draw a star next to your best writing. Think about your fluency and speed.

Building fluency

Apple and bran muffins

Focus on your fluency as you copy these ingredients.

Ingredients

2 cups self-raising flour, sifted

$\frac{1}{2}$ teaspoon baking powder, sifted

1 cup wheat bran

2 tablespoons brown sugar

1 teaspoon ground cinnamon

1 large pink lady apple, grated

1 cup skim milk

2 eggs, lightly beaten

2 tablespoons vegetable oil

$\frac{1}{2}$ cup apple sauce

Practise your keyboarding skills by typing this recipe procedure.

Place flour, baking powder, bran, sugar, cinnamon and apple in a large bowl. Stir to combine. Make a well in the centre. Place milk, eggs, oil and apple sauce into a jug and whisk until just combined. Pour mixture into well and stir gently. Scoop the batter into the muffin tin. Bake for 15 minutes at 170 degrees Celsius. You will be able to smell when they are cooked.

Consolidating

Copy these sentences to practise your speed and fluency.

Dylan Alcott is an Australian wheelchair tennis player and disability advocate. He is known for his remarkable achievements in wheelchair tennis and his efforts to promote inclusivity for people with disabilities.

Cathy Freeman is a track and field athlete who is celebrated as one of Australia's greatest sporting heroes. She is an Olympic gold medallist who lit the Olympic flame in Sydney. Freeman's athletic skill and unwavering determination have earned her a special place in Australian hearts.

Shane Warne was inducted into the Sport Australia Hall of Fame in 2009 for his contribution to cricket. He transformed the art of leg spin, a type of spin bowling. Warne's impact on cricket was immense and he remains a cricketing legend in Australia.

Assessment: Speed and fluency

Rewrite the words below, using cursive writing.

triumph legend challenge achievement recognition

celebrate skilful potential excellence heritage

Practise your cursive handwriting by copying this information about Sir Donald Bradman.

Sir Donald Bradman was inducted into the Sport Australia Hall of Fame in 1985. On that occasion, he said that if anyone deserves a statue, they should be someone who has lived their life with dignity, integrity, courage and modesty. These qualities are in addition to their skill, and are compatible with pride, ambition and competitiveness.

Teacher feedback

Practise your keyboarding skills by typing this passage.

Fluency and legibility

Spacing

It is important to keep your spacing even between letters and words. This will help to make your writing more legible.

sporting champions

Copy the text below. Remember that tall letters and capitals are the same height. Numerals are the same height as short letters.

Some types of motorsports include the 1000 km touring car race Bathurst 1000 and the Australian Grand Prix, an annual motor racing event. Drivers have to be very fit to cope with the force on the car and their bodies as they drive at such fast speeds. These sporting events provide exciting and thrilling experiences for both participants and spectators.

Fine motor skills task: Copy the drawing.

Size

I am successful when I can:

- ❑ sit with my back straight
- ❑ hold the pencil or pen correctly
- ❑ position my paper
- ❑ make my letters even in size and keep them between the lines.

Learning intention:
To practise sizing letters correctly and keeping letters between the lines

Focus on keeping your letter size between the lines, as it helps to make your writing easier to read.

Practise your cursive handwriting.

Tennis is not only a competitive sport but also a popular recreational activity and a fun way to stay physically active.

The Australian Open is a Grand Slam tournament held annually in Melbourne. Wheelchair tennis follows the same rules as traditional tennis but with a few changes to assist players using wheelchairs. It promotes inclusivity, giving individuals with mobility impairments an opportunity to participate in an active and competitive sport.

Slope

Learning intention: To practise sloping letters correctly, using a slope grid

Keeping the slope of your writing consistent will make your writing easier to read. Use the slope grids below to help you maintain a consistent slope. Copy these words in the space.

recreation

improvement

technique

perseverance

strength

flexibility

Fine motor skills task: Using these images, create a drawing that reminds you of being active, relaxing or doing something you really enjoy in the outdoors.

Developing your signature

Below are some examples of signature styles.

Signature Signature Signature

Everyone needs to put their signature on various documents. Signatures are used when you are signing important documents, such as work forms, letters and certificates. It is important that your signature be unique and easy to write.

Practise your signature below. Try out a few different versions.

Select your favourite version and keep practising it below, so that it becomes automatic.

Using 8 mm single lines

In Year 6, you will write on single lines. Let's get started here, as we practise punctuation. Commas are punctuation marks used in writing to separate items in a list or to indicate a pause in a sentence.

Copy the sentences below to practise using commas.

Beach volleyball

Beach volleyball is one of the most popular recreational activities in the world. It became an Olympic sport at the 1996 games, held in Atlanta, Georgia, in the USA.

Skiing

Skiing is popular in places with snowy climates such as Norway, Canada, Switzerland and Italy. There are many types of skiing, including downhill, alpine and cross-country skiing.

Table tennis

Table tennis, which is similar to ping-pong, is popular in many Asian countries, including China, Vietnam and the Philippines. It is played indoors and is a fast-paced game.

Consolidating

Copy the words in the spaces below and consolidate maintaining consistent slope.

batsman wickets pitch innings

fielding stumps international boundary

Rewrite the following words with the appropriate spacing between the letters.

bowlers run out delivery dismissal tournament

Copy the sentences below, and then check the size of your letters.

Cricket is one of Australia's favourite outdoor sports, with matches lasting from a few hours to several days. It is a sport that requires endurance, skill and strategy.

Self-assessment

Use two stars and a wish strategy to write two things about your work you did well, and one thing that could be improved.

Assessment: Fluency and legibility

Copy the text below, focusing on your size, spacing and slope.

Softball is a team sport that involves two opposing teams hitting a pitched ball and running around a series of bases to reach home plate. A run is scored when a baserunner safely touches all three bases and reaches home plate. Each team has nine players, each of whom gets a turn to bat and to field.

Softball is a sport played by all ages and skill levels throughout Australia. Softball is similar to baseball, but the field is smaller, the ball is bigger and only underhand pitches are allowed.

Fine motor skills task: Select two of your favourite pictures and sketch them in the box below.

Teacher feedback

Practise your keyboarding skills by typing this passage.